A MARVEL GRAPHIC NOVEL™

STARSTRUCK™

THE LUCKLESS, THE ABANDONED, AND THE FORSAKED

by Elaine Lee and Michael Wm. Kaluta

Lettering
Todd Klein

Editors
Archie Goodwin,
Margaret Clark,
Jo Duffy

Editor-in-Chief
James Shooter

**published by
THE MARVEL COMICS GROUP
387 Park Avenue South
New York, New York 10016**

ISBN #0-87135-001-7

INTRODUCTION
by Elaine Lee

I REMEMBER IT LIKE IT WAS YESTERDAY....

but it was really October, 1979 when I met Michael Kaluta in a restaurant on 92nd and Broadway in N.Y.C. "Hi! You girls science fiction fans?" The big, bearded man shuffled uncomfortably, "I'm a fantasy artist." My sister, Susan leaned over and whispered in my ear, "Probably a cab driver who draws in his spare time." I don't know, the guy just looked too ill at ease to be throwing us a line. We exchanged numbers. I filed Michael on a 5x7 card that read: Kaluta/Artist/May be of help on next play.

IN THE BEGINNING WAS THE PLAY.

December 1979 in brief: I ran across a copy of THE STUDIO and was blown away by Kaluta's work. I sent him complimentary tickets for **The Contamination of The Kokomo Lounge,** a play about booze, Jesus, and chemical accidents that my sister and I had written and were acting in. He finally made it there closing night and was, he claims, likewise blown away. He stuck around to yak while we were striking the set. He got the bug and offered to do the poster (no charge!) for our company's next production, a very silly science-fiction comedy soon to be titled **Starstruck**! He gradually got suckered into doing the sets and costumes as well. So began our friendship and our journey through Anarchera.

LET THERE BE COMICS.

While we were working on the play, Michael and I would often find ourselves speculating on the possible pasts and futures of our characters. We decided we would like to do a book together. Our idea was to take several of the characters and, based on things that were revealed about their pasts in the play, recreate the incidents that changed them, made them the kind of creatures they were, set them on the road that would lead them to the confrontation around which the play was built. This is the book. These are the stories.

TO FRIENDS OF STARSTUCK IN ALL ITS FORMS:

Back in the summer of 1980, the major companies weren't doing graphic novels. Sal Quartucio (SQ Productions) kept us alive while we worked on **Starstruck** and was responsible for its publication in Europe and eventually in **Heavy Metal.** Our thanks, Sal. We would also like to thank Julie Simmons-Lynch for her support and the terrific article on the play (HM, May 83) and Kip Gould of Broadway Play Publishing for getting the play out there. A very contented type thanks goes to Jim Shooter and Archie Goodwin for taking a chance on us and giving us all that wonderful money for doing the thing we love most.

Our thanks also to composer Dwight Dixon, the man who brought sound to the **Starstruck** universe. If you think **Starstruck** looks good, you should have heard it! A tip of the hat to Charles Vess for helping us to realize Michael's designs for the play. Finally, our thanks to the actors who became the characters for us: Paul Ratkevitch (Kalif Bajar), Karen Bebb (Erotica Ann), Sandra Spurney (Verloona), Neal Ashmun (Rah El Rex), Kathy Gerber (Sister Bronwyn of the Cosmic Veil), and lastly and mostly my co-authors on the play Susan, my crazy sister who was, is, and always will be Brucilla and Dale Place, my ex-husband but all-time friend (Awww, gee whiz!) who breathed the soul into Dwannyun of Grivarr.

Dedicated to Robert Altman and Thomas Pynchon

CYCLE 88 ANARCHERA

SOMEWHERE IN THE DEPTHS OF SPACE...

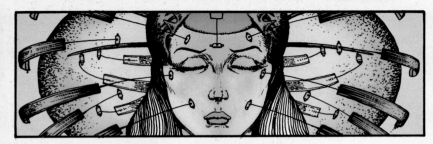

ILLUSION... SOMETIMES CONFUSED WITH ALLUSION.

ILLUSION: AN UNREAL IMAGE OR MISLEADING APPEARANCE.
ALLUSION: AN INDIRECT REFERENCE.

STARSTRUCK

BOOK ONE –
THE LUCKLESS, THE ABANDONED, AND FORSAKED

PLOT BY ELAINE LEE AND M.W. KALUTA
WRITTEN BY ELAINE LEE
ILLUSTRATED BY M.W. KALUTA

BASED UPON THE STAGE PLAY BY ELAINE LEE, NORFLEET LEE, AND DALE PLACE

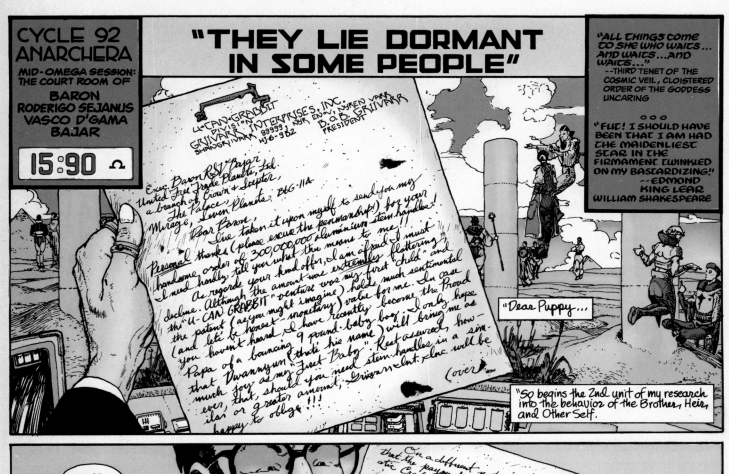

THE EVANGELICALS, SIR... MARCH BAPTISTS FROM ONOLO LINE.

HAVE THEM WAIT IN THE ANTE... NO... BETTER HAVE THEM SHOWN TO THEIR ROOMS... I'LL MEET WITH THEM IN THE UPPER OFFICE BEFORE DINNER.

AND FIND KALIF!

THAT BOY WILL BE THE DEATH OF ME.

"Goal: to gain insight into that quality of "MALENESS" which I lack utterly...

"...and lacking am less thought of than my twin's dim image in a hallway mirror carelessly passed.

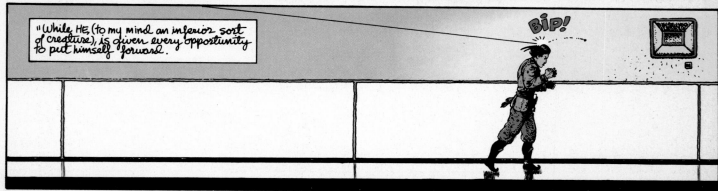

"While HE (to my mind an inferior sort of creature), is given every opportunity to put himself forward.

BIP!

SIR, THE GUY'S FOR REAL. ABSOLUTELY.

NOBODY'S THAT NAIVE... OFFER HIM A PLANET.

HE'S GOT THREE, SIR.

"For the purpose of this experiment, I am using myself as Control since I am the norm...

"... and HE the deviation.

TAKE A LETTER...

THE BARONET PHILLIPE CESARE KALIF ALEXANDER BAJAR.

"TO THE PRESIDENT OF THE COLLECTED GALACTIC SHEET METAL AND MINE WORKERS--" ETC., ETC....

"EVALUATION OF REFLEXES...

"HE responds with mild disgust to the type of minor irritation that provokes CONTROL beyond reason...

"DEAR MADAM..."

"...I REQUIRE SOME INFORMATION ON ONE OF YOUR FORMER MEMBERS-- LAST NAME, GRIIVARR, B_"

SPLOOSH!!

"...resulting in revenge behavior of the most destructive sort.

WE CAN OVERLOOK THE GRADE POINT AVERAGE IF HIS ACHIEVEMENT TESTS ARE ...

LET ME ASSURE YOU, THERE WILL BE NO PROBLEM ON THAT SCORE ... ≈chuckle≈

...MORE COFFEE?

YES, PLEASE.

BARON, IF YOU'LL PERMIT ME.

WE AT THE AMERCADIAN SPACE ACADEMY WOULD HAVE NO PROBLEM WITH YOUR SON'S TEST SCORES OR GRADES IF THE BOY HAS ANYTHING OF HIS DAD IN HIM.

WE ADMIT CADETS ALMOST SOLELY ON THE BASIS OF THE PERSONAL INTERVIEW. WE'RE LOOKING FOR YOUNG PEOPLE WITH STRENGTH OF CHARACTER AND LEADERSHIP ABILITY.

UHM ...

...WAS YOUR SON EVER IN THE RANGERS?

AMBROSIA? WAS KALIF EVER ...?

OF COURSE, ROD, CLASS A-OK!

WELL, WELL ... I'D CERTAINLY LIKE TO MEET THE YOUNG MAN. WILL HE B ...

MY SISTER SAYS SHE'S GLAD SHE DOESN'T HAVE TWO PRUNEY PINK THINGS HANGING DOWN THERE GETTING IN THE WAY. IT'S VERY EMBARRASSING WHEN SHE SAYS THINGS LIKE THAT BECAUSE ...

"Oh, Puppy....!"

...PLEASE DON'T MENTION THIS TO ANYONE -- OH, I KNOW, AND I DO TRUST YOU, BUT PLEASE DON'T MENTION THIS ... IT'S VERY EMBARRASSING ...BECAUSE I'M NOT REALLY SURE *WHAT* SHE HAS IF SHE DOESN'T HAVE -- YOU KNOW ...

I MEAN I HAVE SORT OF A VAGUE IDEA. I'VE HEARD RUMORS--BUT...

...WELL.... I GUESS I WAS SORT OF HOPING THAT-- WHEN WE GOT TO KNOW EACH OTHER BETTER, YOU WOULD-- WELL--IT'S UP TO YOU, OF COURSE--

-- I WAS HOPING YOU MIGHT SATISFY MY CURIOSITY ABOUT THIS THING.

"Something has changed.

"Something has...

NO, NO, NO... IT'S JUST THAT I'VE RECENTLY TAKEN AN INTEREST IN EMERGING YOUNG PLAYWRIGHTS...

...ESPECIALLY IF THEY'RE *EXCITED* BY THINGS OF A *CLASSICAL* NATURE? HO HO HO HO

FORGET IT, DARLING, HE'S INTO WOMEN.

THAT'S *NOT* THE KIND OF INVESTMENT I'M TALKING ABOUT--

THAT LAST ONE MADE A BUNDLE.

WHAT'S THE NAME OF HIS LATEST?

"AREIOPAGITICA"

OH, GOD! THEY'LL ALL BE WEARING TOGAS NEXT CY...

I TRIED ASKING DAD ABOUT THIS, BUT HE SAID ALL I NEEDED TO KNOW WAS THAT WHEN I GOT OLD ENOUGH TO FEEL LIKE DOING IT...

...AND AGAIN, I'M A LITTLE VAGUE ON THE DETAILS...

...THAT I SHOULD TRY VERY HARD TO GET THE GIRL TO PUT IT IN HER MOUTH...

...BUT THAT I SHOULD NEVER, *UNDER ANY CIRCUMSTANCES*, PUT *HERS* IN MY MOUTH.

THIS HAS ADDED GREATLY TO MY CONFUSION AS I DIDN'T THINK GIRLS HAD ANY.

MAYBE YOU COULD CLEAR THIS UP FOR ME.

WOULD YOU LIKE TO PUT IT IN YOUR MOUTH?

OH -- EXCUSE ME -- I FORGET MYSELF.

MY SISTER WRITES SPECULATIVE FICTION WHICH DAD SAYS IS A WASTE OF TIME, AND I AGREE. MY THEORY IS THAT, SINCE SHE DOESN'T HAVE BALLS, SHE HAS HAD TO FIND SOMETHING ELSE TO DO WITH HER LIFE.

WITH THAT KIND OF CREDIT, WE COULD BUILD OUR TABERNACLE AND LAUNCH THE ONOLO DOS MISSION, TOO!

VERY KIND OF THE BARON, BUT I CAN'T HELP WONDERING...

THE LORD WORKS IN MYSTERIOUS WAYS.

AND IF HE SHOULD ASK US...?

"RENDER UNTO CAESAR"

I TRIED TO TOUCH MY SISTER'S BREAST ONCE--

I SNUCK INTO HER ROOM WHILE SHE WAS SLEEPING AND TRIED TO TOUCH ONE, BUT SHE WAS JUST PRETENDING TO BE ASLEEP, AND RIGHT WHEN I WAS NEARLY TOUCHING IT SHE SAT STRAIGHT UP AND SCREAMED,

"WHY SHOULD I LET A LOATHSOME LITTLE TOAD LIKE YOU TOUCH MY BREAST WHEN YOU HAVEN'T EVEN READ MY BOOKS!"

AND I THREW UP.

"Evaluation of reflexes...

DAD FOUND OUT AND DIDN'T SPEAK TO ME FOR THREE MALTON UNITS.

HE SAID HE COULD HAVE NOTHING TO DO WITH A SON WHO HAD NO MORE BALLS THAN THAT.

THIS KIND OF TALK MAKES ME VERY NERVOUS.

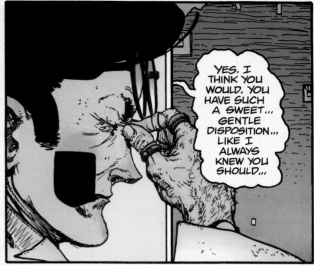

YES. I THINK YOU WOULD. YOU HAVE SUCH A SWEET... GENTLE DISPOSITION... LIKE I ALWAYS KNEW YOU SHOULD...

TAKE A LETTER...

"All things come to she who waits...

"...and waits... and waits...

TO 'LIVING DOLL' CYBERNETICS... ETC., ETC.... GROMMIT-- YOU GOT THE FRANCHISE, BUT I NEED A FAVOR FROM YOU... EROTICA ANDROIDS... AS MANY AS YOU'VE GOT... DON'T BOTHER SENDING ANY OF YOUR OTHER LINES, JUST ANNIES... I NEED ANNIES...

"Theory: This is merely a transition stage (brought on by the loss of the love object) and will ultimately result in some minor alteration of prior patterns.

...POSTHASTE!

"Alternate theory: Boys are very easy to break.

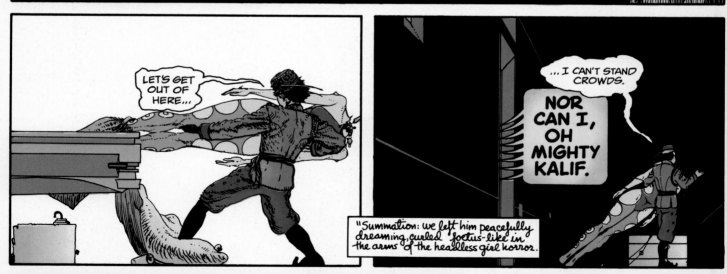

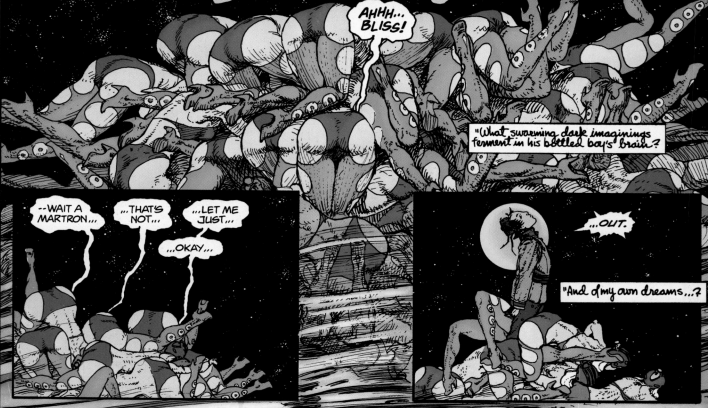

"A STITCH IN TIME..."

CYCLE 93
ANARCHERA
THE FAMILY CRÉCHE
12 OCHS
(FORMERLY THE
BARKLY RANCH)
7 OCHS,
NEW WYOMING

A RIDDLE OF PHYSICS:
THOUGH QUARKS ARE SISTERS,
THEY COME IN DIFFERENT
FLAVORS.
SOME ARE CHARMED.
SOME ARE STRANGE.
SOME HAVE DIRECTION.
THOUGH THEY MAY BE COMPANY,
TWO QUARKS DO NOT A
BARYON MAKE.
ONE WILL CRY.
ONE WILL DIE.
BUT ONLY ONE WILL EVER PSI.
ABSENCE MAKES THE
QUARK GROW FONDER.

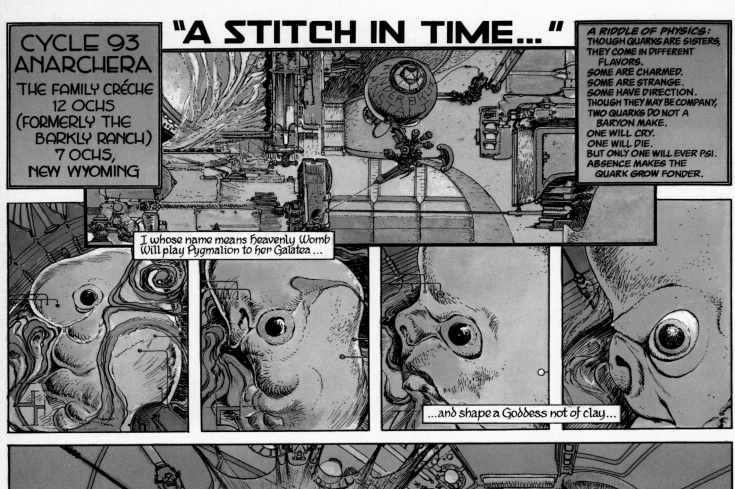

I whose name means Heavenly Womb
Will play Pygmalion to her Galatea...

...and shape a Goddess not of clay...

...but out of dancing atoms and
another's Spiralling DNA.

URP!

Two down. One to go.

CYCLE 94
ANARCHERA
PLAYROOM/WORKSHOP
OF THE BARONET
PHILLIPE CESARE
KALIF ALEXANDER
BAJAR

"GLORIANNA (READ GLORIOUS ANNIE) WAS ONE OF THE *'IN TUNE'*...MOVING WITH THE RHYTHM OF THE UNIVERSE, RIDING HER CURRENTS, APPEARING SIGH-SOFT WHERE OPPORTUNITY KNOCKED."
--FROM THE DIARY OF I.L.R.L.E. BAJAR

"I'M GOING TO BUY A PAPER DOLL THAT I CAN CALL MY OWN, A DOLL THAT OTHER FELLOWS CANNOT STEAL. AND THEN THE FLIRTY,

FLIRTY GUYS WITH FLIRTY, FLIRTY EYES WILL HAVE TO FLIRT WITH DOLLIES THAT ARE REAL. WHEN I COME HOME AT NIGHT SHE

WILL BE WAITING, SHE'LL BE THE TRUEST DOLL IN ALL THIS WORLD. I'D RATHER HAVE A PAPER DOLL TO CALL MY OWN THAN

TO HAVE A FICKLE-MINDED REAL LIVE GIRL."   LYRICS AND MELODY BY JOHNNY S. BLACK ©1942

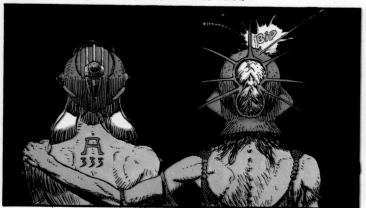

"MUMBO-JUMBO!"

CYCLE 132
ANARCHERA

OMEGA: DISQUE 6,
AUTOMATED FARMING
DISQUE AND PENAL
COLONY BUILT BY
GALATIAL FIBER FEED
& FERMENTING,
IER-CO (DEFUNCT)
ABANDONED AFTER
THE OVERTHROW OF
THE INCORPORATED
ELYSIAN REPUBLIC,
CYCLE 1 ANARCHERA.

HEH! HEH! YOR ASS N'MAH FACE!

WHUDYOO SAY?

"WHOSE CRY BEYOND THE PORTAL?"

"So shut your eyes while mother sings
Of wonderful sights that be,
And you shall see the beautiful things
As you rock in the misty sea,
Where the old shoe rocked the fishermen three:
Wynken,
Blynken,
And Nod."

--EUGENE FIELD,
POEMS OF CHILDHOOD

AH SEHD, WHUD'YOO SAY, BOY?

AH SEHD YOO GODDA FACE LAHK TH'UNNASAHV UFFA PIG'S BUTT.

"IT IS I, GALATIA, CHILD OF THE VOID..."

LISTEN TO THE 9th TAEL OF TRIVIA

SHUT Y'HOLE FO'AH PLUG IT FOE YUH!

"...THE MOTHER'S STARRY WOMB."

T'WAS IN THE AGE OF DARKNESS WHEN OUR ENEMIES HELD THE SACRED SEED CHAMBERS

SONUFFA ASS, BOOTIN' SQUIT!

"KNOW THEN, GALATIA, THAT YOU TREAD UPON THE TESTING GROUND BEFORE THE DOOR TO THE KINGDOM OF DEATH..."

T'WAS IN THE AGE OF DARKNESS WHEN THE MAIDEN FELL, A SMALL STAR, FROM THE SKY

BANG!

T'WAS IN THAT AGE THAT MAIDEN, BOW, AND SISTERS BECAME AS ONE HAND, SMITING THE DEADLY DROMES

© 1981 Elaine Lee
McSugura

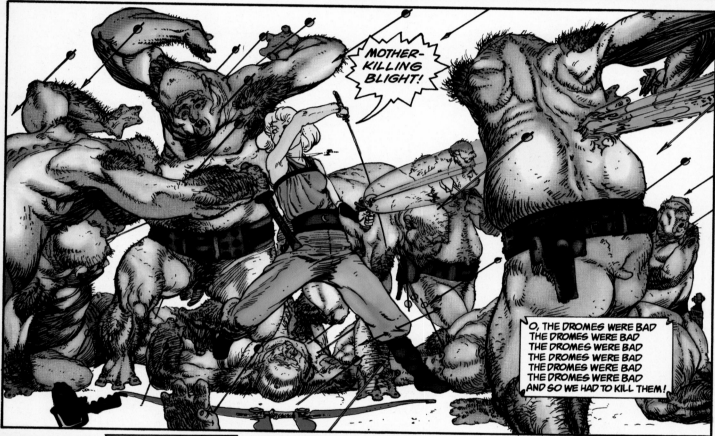

NAWWWW... L'TUL SUGUH BRITCHIZ WOOD'N DO DIS T'OLE...

URK!

BUZZATT

BUZZATT

BUZZATT

9 MARTRONS, NOT TOO SHODDY!

SO ARE YOU BROUGHT INTO THE CIRCLE!

I ENTER THE CIRCLE IN PERFECT LOVE AND PERFECT TRUST...

GALATIA 9!

STAR MOTHER! KEEPER OF THE NIGHT! BEHOLD YOUR DAUGHTER, GALATIA 9, WHO IS NOW MADE SISTER AND AMAZON!

...FOUND THE STILL!

AWRIGHT!

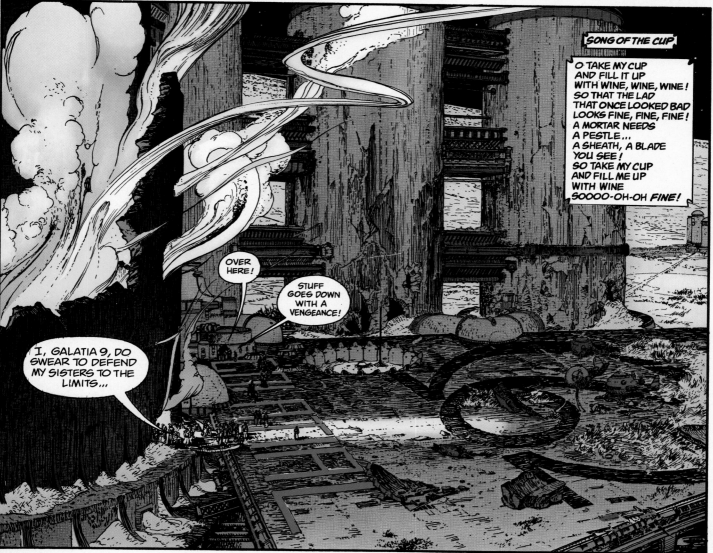

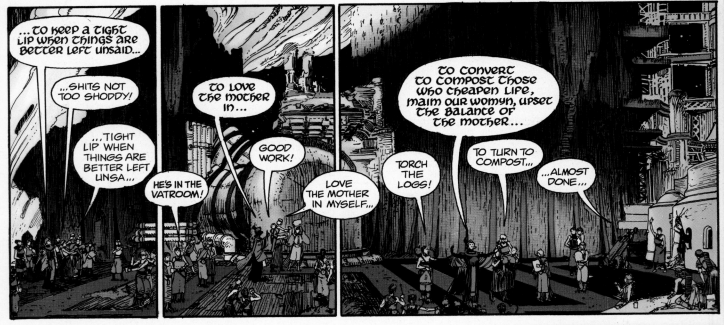

...TO KEEP A TIGHT LIP WHEN THINGS ARE BETTER LEFT UNSAID...

...SHITS NOT TOO SHODDY!

...TIGHT LIP WHEN THINGS ARE BETTER LEFT UNSA...

HE'S IN THE VATROOM!

TO LOVE THE MOTHER IN...

GOOD WORK!

LOVE THE MOTHER IN MYSELF...

TO CONVERT TO COMPOST THOSE WHO CHEAPEN LIFE, MAIM OUR WOMYN, UPSET THE BALANCE OF THE MOTHER...

TORCH THE LOGS!

TO TURN TO COMPOST...

...ALMOST DONE...

HO! HAVE YOU GOT THE BOY OILED AND READY?

...UPSET THE BALANCE OF THE MOTHER...

GALA·A·A·TIA!!

PUT ONE HAND UNDER YOUR FEET AND ONE OVER YOUR HEAD AND REPEAT:

THIS I SWEAR ON MY MOTHER'S WOMB, THE BLOOD OF MY HEART, AND ON ANY LIVES THAT MIGHT BE MINE UPON THE END OF THIS WOMON SPAN, AND IF I BREAK THIS OATH, ...

BLOOD IN MY HEART AND ON MY... shit.

...LET MY LOT BE WORSE THAN THE LOTS OF THOSE WHO LIVED IN THE BURNING TIMES, ONLY WORSE IN THE KNOWLEDGE THAT I BROUGHT THIS GHASTLY FATE DOWN UPON MY OWN HEAD, AND LET MY BLADE TURN AGAINST ME. SO BE IT.

ALL BETWEEN PALM AND PALM BELONGS TO THE MOTHER.

SONG OF THE EARTH BORN STAR...

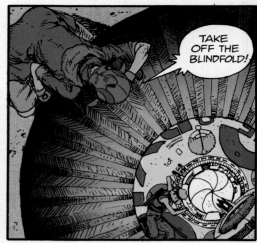

AND MUCH TO OUR SURPRISE
WHEN WE OPENED UP OUR EYES
WE WERE SAYING OUR GOODBYES
FOR THE LADY SPREAD HER THIGHS
AND A STAR WAS BORN
YES A STAR WAS BORN
A TINY STAR WAS BORN
YES, A STAR WAS BORN OF EARTH

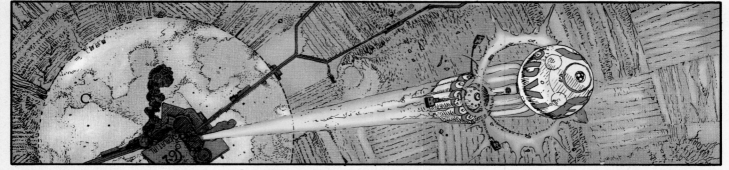

OH DEAR...

...UM...

...UH...

LET IT BE WRITTEN!

...THE CIRCLE SPINS COMPLETE...

"...AND OUR MAIDEN SWEET BOW-BRINGER, STAR-BORN FIRE-SEED WHITE...

"...HAVING SHARED OUR FIGHT, RETURNS TO THE SKY FROM WHENCE SHE FELL...

"...TO SHARE HER LOVELY LIGHT!

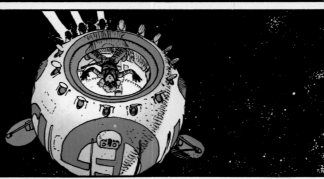

"O, FIRE SEED QUICKEN...!

"...FLAME...

"...BLAZE!

"...AND BURNING BRIGHT EMBRACE NOT MAN BUT LOVING NIGHT...

"...SHINE! GALATIA 9!"

SO SPEAKS TRIVIA.

I THINK I'M GONNA BE SICK.

THE VOID

...IF YOU INSIST ON...

YOU REALLY SHOULD TRY ONE OF THESE, MAHKINA!

THANK YOU VERY MUCH NO. NOW... WHERE ...?

num !!!

"WE THREE KINGS OF ORIENT ARE. TRIED TO SMOKE A RUBBER CISAR. IT WAS LOADED AND EXPLODED... SILENT NIGHT ..."
--OBSCURE RHYME ATTRIBUTED TO THE CHILDREN OF EARTH.

OH YES...!

IF YOU INSIST ON TALKING ABOUT TOTALLY NONSEXUAL ENERGY SPONTANEOUSLY COMBUSTING IN A VACUUM INTO A NORMALLY HUNG HUMANOID, YOU CAN JUST BE THAT WAY!

I DID!

YOU DIDN'T!

could you die!

HE HAD A FIT?

THREATENED TO CALL THE UNION.

OH NO!

ha-ha-ha-ha...

..ha-ha-ha-ha...!

ISN'T IT, THOUGH! ...MORE DRINK, PERSONUS?

PLEASE.

oh-h-h-h-h-h..., ≥sigh≤
≥SIGH≤ ... ME, TOO.
THE QUIET BEFORE THE STORM BEFORE THE QUIET.
ha-ha-ha-ha...!
DON'T TRY SO HARD, EX...THE CAMERA'S ALWAYS LOVED YOU!
i don't think i know what...
YOU KNOW PERFECTLY WELL, DON'T BE ...
silly, i know...

WHOMP!

IRRELEVANT!

WHAT? CLIK

FLUFF! THE PIECE WAS FLUFF! THE MATERIAL. ART FOR THE SAKE OF *AR...*

SHHHHHH!

"WHAT GOOD A PRETTY VERSE TO ME, MY POLITICS ARE POETRY." PARDON... ALL GREAT *A-T* IS POLITICAL.

"ALL A-T IS SPIRITUAL... THE REVOLUTIONARY ACT." CLIK CLIK

HO...

THAT'S PRECISELY WHY WE SEEK THE END. CLIK WRRRR

OMEGA.

fini.

COME AGAIN?

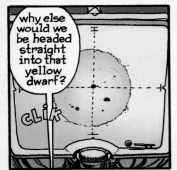

why else would we be headed straight into that yellow dwarf? CLIK

WHAT?

FIND GLORY!

KNOW GRACE!

suffer for the sins of an uninspired director!

NOT WITH *ME* YOU DON'T!

THERE'S LITTLE YOU CAN DO...

It'S BEEN DECIDED.

BZZZZ

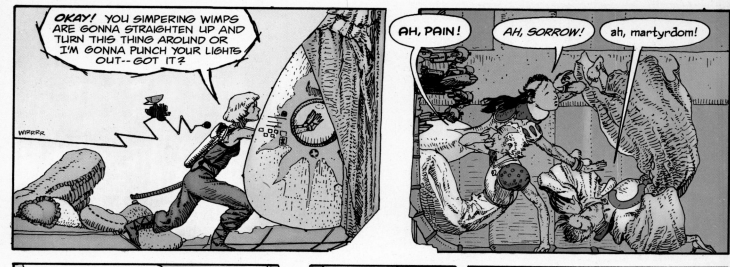

OKAY! YOU SIMPERING WIMPS ARE GONNA STRAIGHTEN UP AND TURN THIS THING AROUND OR I'M GONNA PUNCH YOUR LIGHTS OUT-- GOT IT?

WIRRRR

AH, PAIN!

AH, SORROW!

ah, martyrdom!

...NOT THE WAY TO GO WITH THIS THING...

SLAM!

I'M ONLY DOING THIS FOR YOUR SAKE GUYS. HEY...! YOU KIDS HAD YOUR LITTLE HEARTS SET ON MEETING ETERNITY AS A TRINITY?

I MAKE FOUR.

FOUR'S A QUARTET.

A PROBLEM. true. WE HADN'T CONSIDERED.

THERE IS A SOLUTION THAT I BELIEVE WOULD MEET WITH YOUR UNANIMOUS APPROVAL. IF I MAY?

CeRTa/NEmENt.

HERE'S THE SCOOP: THE THREE OF YOU HEAD FOR THE NEAREST HANDY ESCAPE POD AND TAKE OFF STRAIGHT OUT OF THE GALAXY LIKE A BAT OUTA HELL. SO... YOU'LL BE GOING FASTER AND FASTER, AND AS YOU GET CLOSER TO THE SPEED OF LIGHT, TIME REVERSES AND YOU'RE GOIN BACK FURTHER AND FURTHER, AND WHEN YOU REACH LIGHT-SPEED...

BAM!!!ooo

...YOU BECOME PURE ENERGY, MERGE, BECOME LIGHT, THREE BEINGS IN ONE, PRE-CREATION, PREGNANT WITH POSSIBILITY... IN A WORD: GOD!

JOY!

RAPTURE!

the pinnacle, craft-wise.

"DEAD RECKONING"

CYCLE 134
ANARCHERA

VARIOUS POINTS
OF INTEREST
AROUND THE
CIVILIZED UNIVERSE

YOU'RE *SURE* ABOUT THAT? HMMMMMM. THAT'S INTERESTING. THANKS.

YOU BET YOUR *BOOTS*, BARON OLE BUDDY! THIS ONE'S IN THE HOLDING BAY... AND MAKE THAT *STANDARD* CREDITS.

YOU'VE GOT A *BET*, WEATHERAL... 20,000 IT IS... IN... UH...STANDARD CREDITS.

FIND OUT WHAT'S UP AND THEN STOP IT! I DON'T PLAN TO LOSE ANOTHER BET WITH "WINDBAG" WEATHERAL.

CERTAINLY, DEAR FATHER. I HAVE A FRIEND... A FRATERNITY BROTHER. HE SHOULD BE DELIGHTED TO HELP US OUT.

IF THIS IS TRUE...YOU BET YOUR SWEET ASS I'LL HELP. IF WE CAN'T WIN FAIR AND SQUARE, WE'LL LOSE BIG TIME.

THAT'S RIGHT, POP... I *HEAR* THERE'S A WRENCH IN THE WORKS -- *IF-YOU-KNOW-WHAT-I-MEAN?* NOTHING THAT ISN'T FIXABLE. JUST MAKE SURE I'M NAMED ATTACK CO-ORDINATER, THEN LEAVE IT TO ME.

I DON'T WANT TO KNOW *ANYTHING* ABOUT THIS, SON. DO WHAT YOU HAVE TO.

IT'S DONE, DAD.

"... an order that would change the course of my life... an order on which would turn (indirectly) the fate of the free universe... an order I was told would be a piece of cake..."

"We were ordered to make a run thru the off-limits NEUTRAL ZONE 8 (my bones turned to mega-jelly)... to elude the vitrolic VERCADIAN PROTECTOR ANDROIDS (my blood turned to H_2O)... and to EGG SAINT ARNOLD ZAPOROFFSKY'S MILITARY PEP BAND as they played on PORT-O-BOY GAZEBO 16."

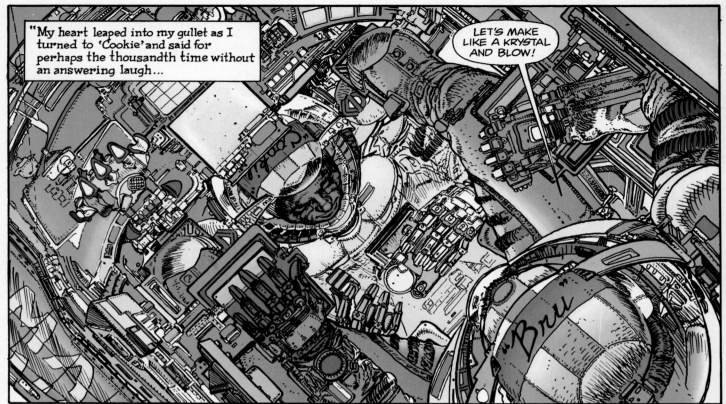

"My heart leaped into my gullet as I turned to 'Cookie' and said for perhaps the thousandth time without an answering laugh...

"As 'Cookie' whipped a 200-vilo batch of imitation powdered egg substitute into the ship's evacuation hopper (with which to soufflé said pep band), I fielded the ribald chatter from my brave squadron-mates as we hurtled toward our appointment with destiny!

"And before you could say 'up the brigade' we found ourselves entering the more than usually deadly NEUTRAL ZONE 8...

WARNING!!! YOU ARE NOW ENTERING NEUTRAL ZONE 8. VANISH OR BE VAPORIZED!

UP YOURS, TOOTS, WE'RE COMIN' THRU!

" I had the best of gunnery sergeants, my squadron was 'A' number one and my hardware was state o' the art. We're talkin' DEVASTATION! I ran my eyes across the tactical screens: there were no wallflowers in my bunch...no one haulin' any dead wood... our attack pattern was as tight as a paymaster's fist.

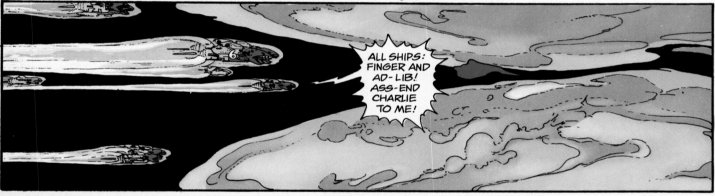

ALL SHIPS: FINGER AND AD-LIB! ASS-END CHARLIE TO ME!

HANG TIGHT, COOKIE, WE'LL SHOW THOSE YEAST-FARTS WHAT BRIGADIERS ARE MADE OF!

" I blinked back a tear of pride as I prepared for the first onslaught of coherent hell-fire from the Vercadian bases."

"The voices of the brave lads and lasses of Squadron 4, 21st Tactical Assault Group drifted into and were lost in the dark embrace of Mother Void as their ships shrieked into the black bowels of the Neutral Zone."

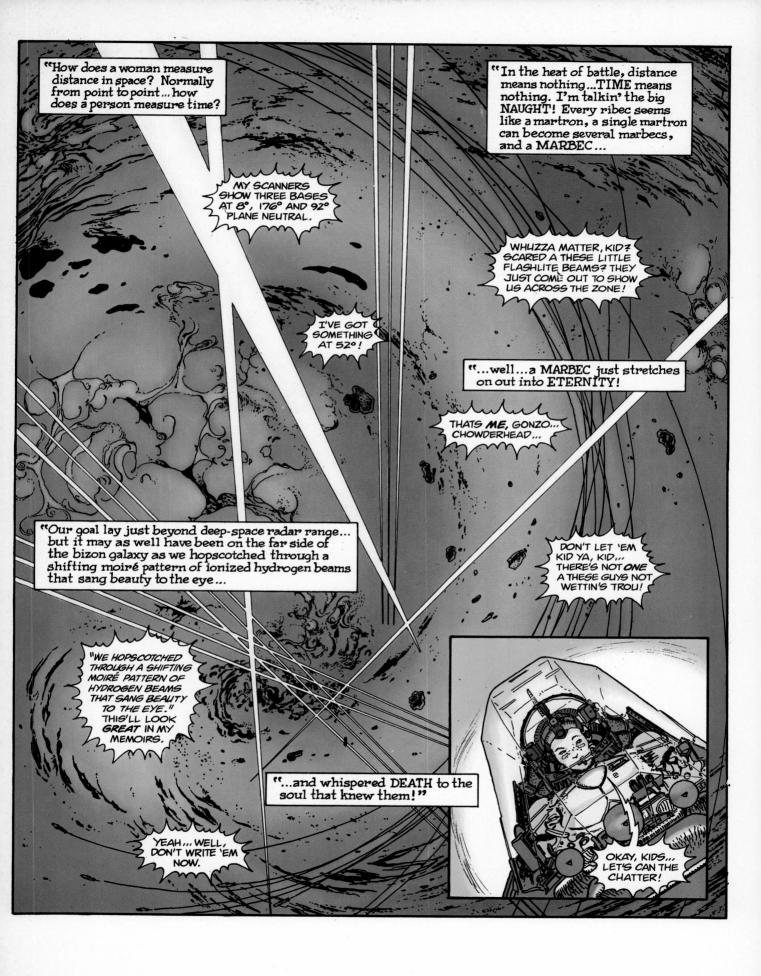

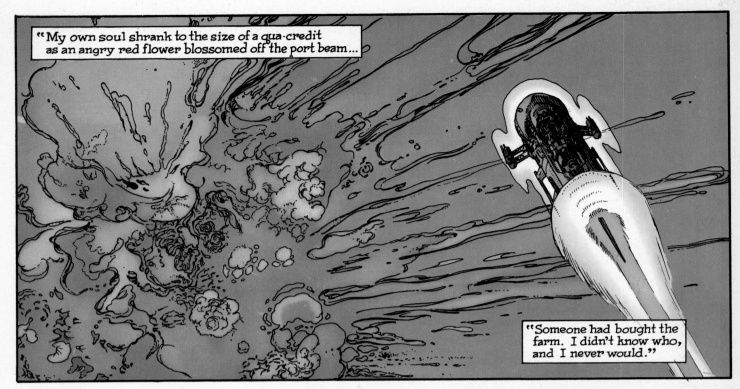

"My own soul shrank to the size of a qua-credit as an angry red flower blossomed off the port beam...

"Someone had bought the farm. I didn't know who, and I never would."

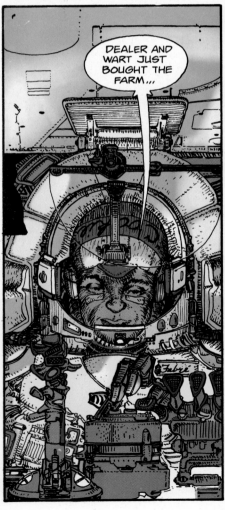

DEALER AND WART JUST BOUGHT THE FARM....

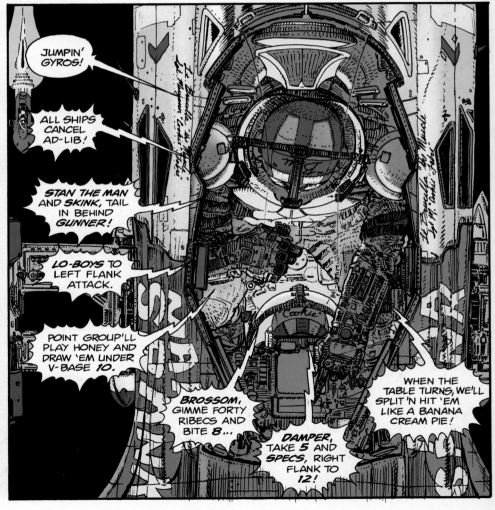

JUMPIN' GYROS!

ALL SHIPS CANCEL AD-LIB!

STAN THE MAN AND SKINK, TAIL IN BEHIND GUNNER!

LO-BOYS TO LEFT FLANK ATTACK.

POINT GROUP'LL PLAY HONEY AND DRAW 'EM UNDER V-BASE 10.

BROSSOM, GIMME FORTY RIBECS AND BITE 8...

DAMPER, TAKE 5 AND SPECS, RIGHT FLANK TO 12!

WHEN THE TABLE TURNS, WE'LL SPLIT 'N HIT 'EM LIKE A BANANA CREAM PIE!

"My lips moved in a silent prayer to the Mother as point group crawled under Vercadian Base 10, drawing their H-beams like so many Pryfromian Phlys. And suddenly...

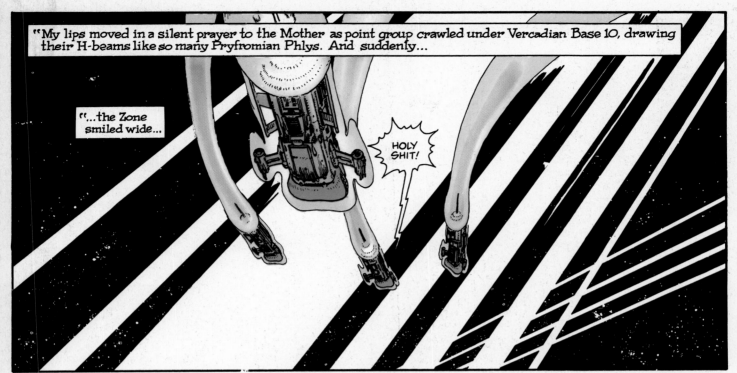

"...the Zone smiled wide...

HOLY SHIT!

"...belching bile from its great churning gut, and each brave Brigader of Point Group saw his or her face reflected in its omnivorous teeth as he or she stared grim-faced down the trembling throat of death!

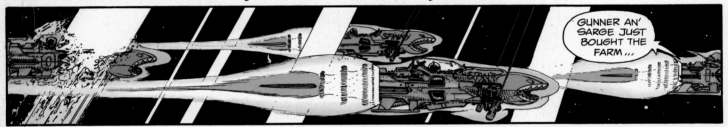

GUNNER AN' SARGE JUST BOUGHT THE FARM...

"Unbeknownst to me, "Damper" and the Hi-Boys had cut out the malignant Base 5 like the cancer it was. My full attention was, at the time, primarily focused on keepin' Point Group clear of the fast-fryin' fangs of the death-dealin' droids.

My full attention proved to be worth less than a BAJAR SHILLING.

SKINK AND WEEBLE JUST BOUGHT THE FARM!

"There was a hell of a lotta real estate auctioned off in that Neutral Zone an' my kids thought they were pickin' it wholesale! To my mind, they were paying top dollar...

"...they were paying with BRIGADER BLOOD!

OH MOTHER OH MOTHER OH MOTHER! STAN...!

"... I saw it comin' at 'em, but before I could say 'Stan! Claw off to Port!', Stan and "Butcher" had been reduced to a fond memory...
...and just as suddenly--"

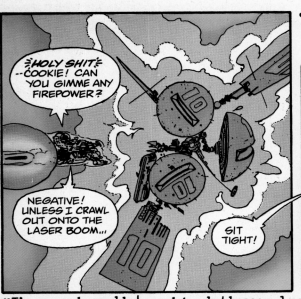

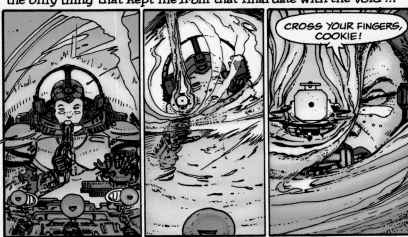

"As we sped toward obliteration, I hoisted myself up in my stirrups, pressing the barrel of my blaster slowly into and thru the translucent field of force whose quivering skin of energy was the only thing that kept me from that final date with the void ..."

"I've never been able to explain what happened next. Suffice it to say...I am here to tell the story...and I never fired my blaster. SOMETHING took out V-base 10...I don't know what...perhaps I never will...

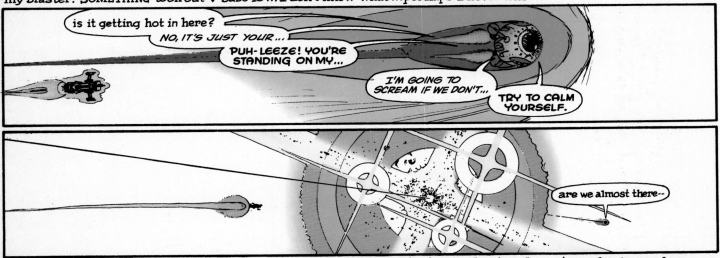

"Before I could breathe the usual sigh of relief, I became aware that we had entered an atmospheric envelope surrounding the ex-V-base. This fact became clear to me when I noticed the condition of the ship!

"... AND, I might add, not a ribec too soon!

WHU HAPPENED?

"The virulent Vercadians, none too happy about Base 10 bein' neutralized, had let go a quasar beam from Base 9 an' reduced Mama Spank to a cloud of dust an' debris no bigger'n a Phryben's sneeze...

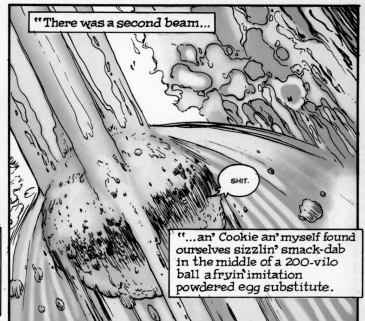

"There was a second beam...

SHIT.

"...an' Cookie an' myself found ourselves sizzlin' smack-dab in the middle of a 200-vilo ball a fryin' imitation powdered egg substitute.

"As we were batted about by the following barrage of beams like krystal braids on a Krabian belly-dancer's hips, I was surprised to hear the familiar bleeping tones of my in-suit communicator... an', shortly after, the sweetest words these ole ears have heard to this malton-unit!

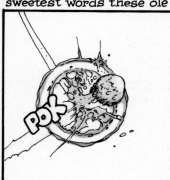

POK

POK

POK

KA POK!

BLEEP: YOU ARE NOW LEAVING NEUTRAL ZONE 8. RETURN AT YOUR OWN RISK!

"What happened next was irony run amok... for where did our makeshift ship o' synthetic egg substitute choose, out of every floating hunk of what-not in the ever-lovin' void...?

"You guessed it! PORT-O-BOY 16!"

"We put a crater in that thing the size of a small swimmin' pool not six BANLONS from St. Arnold's Pep Band!

"The second thing we saw after wipin' the egg off our vizors... (the first bein' the dumb-struck faces of the St. Arnold's Pep Band)...

"...was a giant-sized vi-screen loomin' over us, containin' the giant-sized image of Mother Amy Simple, head honcho of The Cosmic Veil, Cloistered Order of the Goddess Uncaring!

WE ARE NOT AMUSED... TO ERR IS HUMAN, BUT *THIS!* ...THIS WAS NAUGHTY...

...A NO-NO OF THE *GRAVEST* SORT... THE SISTERHOOD FEELS THAT TO *LET* THIS *ACTION*... THE DELIBERATE DISRUPTION OF *PIOUS* SISTERS PURSUING THEIR GODESS-GIVEN *RIGHT* OF RELIGIOUS FREEDOM... TO LET *THIS* GO UNPUNISHED WOULD BE GIVING THE *GREEN LIGHT* TO FUTURE INFRACTIONS OF OUR TREATY.

IN VIEW OF THIS... WE HAVE DECIDED TO WITHDRAW OUR *HANDSOME* SEMI-CYCLE GIFT OF 20,000 MEGACREDITS TO THE AMERCADIAN SPACE ACADEMY.

" It would seem that Mother 'A' had a crimp in her craw due to the fact that the Sisterhood had one of its cosmic hen-coops tucked back in the Neutral Zone, and the commotion caused by Squadron 4's collision with the forces of chaos had disturbed her meditory vibrations.

"This was nothing, however, when compared with the enraged countenance of General "Typhoon" Weatheral appeared shortly thereafter lookin' as if somethin' was gonna rupture..."

GRAB 'EM!

WHO? US?

"The next few marbecs were a nightmare. Little did I suspect that I was to play the pawn in a drama of deception that made a travesty of justice and a mockery of the words 'fair play'.

I'LL BE OUTA HERE IN NO TIME! YOU'RE TALKIN' TO A GAL THAT KNOWS THE MEANIN' OF THE WORDS "BE PREPARED"!

I GOT IT ALL ON RECORD! RIGHT ON THE OLE TAPE-EROO!

HA! THEY'LL EAT THEIR--

"Suffice it to say that yours truly took the brunt of the Brigade Brass's not so righteous wrath.

WHAT!?

"And the tape? The tape was not admitted as evidence. They should'a killed me. They didn't. I was humiliated, cashiered, broken from the ranks.

RRIP! POP POP POP POP SNAP SNAP PLUK PLUK PLUK

"good 'till the last drop"

"'Cookie' got off with a mere 90 cycles a' K.P.

"They marched me out of the courtroom...

"... down deep into and through the dank gray back corridors of Brigade Headquarters. I hung my head, so filled was I with shame and burning rage and then, by yet another foul turn of fate, found myself face to face with the last guy in Amercadia I wanted to run into at this moment."

GEE WHIZ! HI BRU. WHO'RE YOUR FRIENDS?

GOT BAD NEWS FOR YA DWAIN...

ER...THAT'S DWANNYUN.

TONIGHT'S NO GO. I'M GONNA HAFTA BREAK OUR DATE. SORRY KID.

RATTAT TAT TAT

"I CAN'T WAIT UNTIL TOMORROW 'CAUSE I GET BETTER-LOOKIN' EVERY MALTON-UNIT"
The Life and Times of Brucilla "The Muscle": Woman of War ~ Lucky in Love

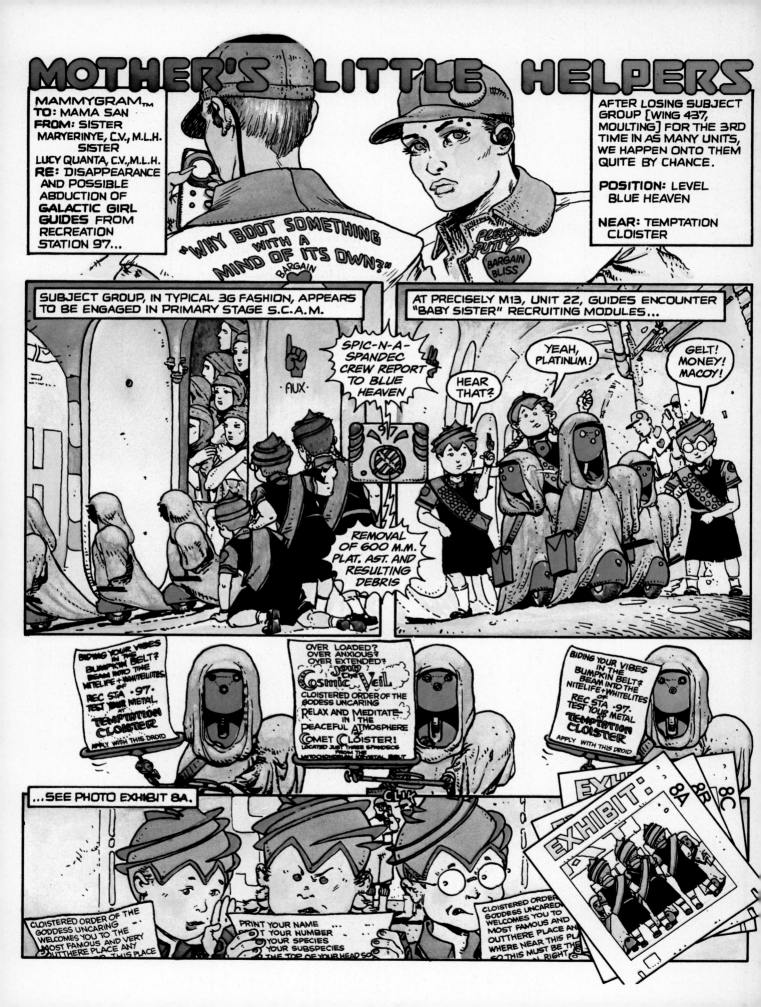

UPON COMPLETION OF INFO TRANSFER MODULES DISENGAGE, PROCEED DOWN RIGHT CORRIDOR TOWARD DISTRIBUTION SECTOR 10/4: "THE GUTTERS". GUIDES IN PURSUIT.

OUR ATTEMPT TO FOLLOW IS IMPEDED BY ACCELERATING "FLOTSAM" IN PROCESS OF ELUDING REC/POLS.

GET THE **HELL** OUTA MY WAY!

WE RECOVER AND PROCEED TOWARD CORRIDOR TO INVESTIGATE SOUNDS WHICH WE INTERPRET AS RECRUITING MODULES ENGAGED IN "RESIST THE DEVIL" DEFENSE MODE. WE ASSUME TERMINATION OF GIRL GUIDE GROUP.

ASSUMPTION CONFIRMED. BABY SISTERS REENGAGE PRIMARY FUNCTION RESUME... SHIT...! BACK UP...

CORRECTION: GUIDES HAVE CUT & RUN
CONCLUSION: MISSION ABORTED
CAUSE: AGENT ERROR

COMMENT:
THE GUIDES TRAINING IS VERY EFFECTIVE. IT IS IMPOSSIBLE TO ASCERTAIN AT THIS TIME WHETHER THE DISAPPEARANCES ARE THE WORK OF SOME OUTSIDE AGENT OR SOME UNKNOWN PLAN OF THE GUIDES THEMSELVES. END REPORT.

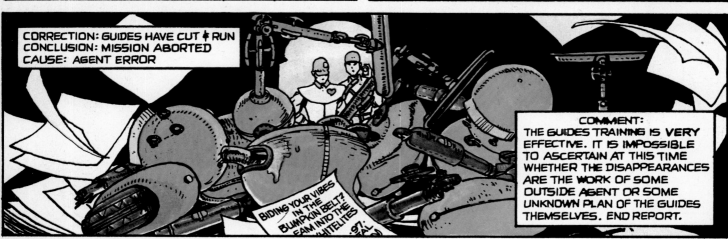

"I ATE A WHOLE FUNNEL CAKE..."

"WHAT YOU DO AT GUN-POINT WILL DEPEND ON BOTH YOUR BASIC NATURE AND THE SPEED OF THE BULLET. WHERE YOU LAND AFTER THE JUMP IS *WHERE YOU ARE!* *WHERE YOU ARE!* IS THE ONLY STARTING POINT YOU HAVE FOR ANY ACT OF FREE WILL. YOU CAN SEE THE CONNECTION."

--FROM *CONVERSATIONS WITH THE GREAT MOTHER* BY BRONWYN, FIFTH-LEVEL SISTER OF THE COSMIC VEIL, CLOISTERED ORDER OF THE GODDESS UNCARING

GRTZ...

AW, GO JUMP UP A HOG'S BUTT AN' GRAB A HAM SANDWICH!

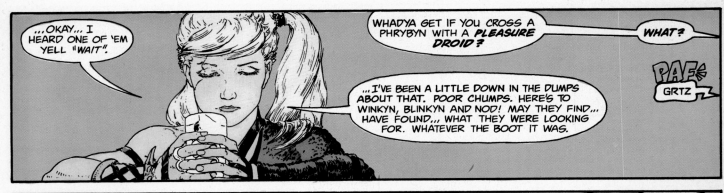

...OKAY... I HEARD ONE OF 'EM YELL "WAIT".

WHADYA GET IF YOU CROSS A PHRYBYN WITH A *PLEASURE DROID?*

WHAT?

PAF GRTZ

...I'VE BEEN A LITTLE DOWN IN THE DUMPS ABOUT THAT. POOR CHUMPS. HERE'S TO WINKYN, BLINKYN AND NOD! MAY THEY FIND... HAVE FOUND... WHAT THEY WERE LOOKING FOR. WHATEVER THE BOOT IT WAS.

...A PHRYBYN WITH A VAT-GROWN FACE AND AN I.Q. OF *THREE!*

WHAZZA MATTER, *STUD?* YOU NEVER SEEN A GOOD-LOOKIN' WOMAN BEFORE?

WELL, KEEP YOUR *PECKER* IN YOUR *PANTS,* I'M NOT INTERESTED!

...SAME TO *YOU,* JACK!

...OH, *YEAH?*

LISTEN,

I TRAVELED THE GALAXY... *DONE, BEEN, SEEN* EVERYTHING THERE IS TO SEE AND I'VE RUN INTO SOME BOOTIN-*STUPID* CUBS-O'-CURS BUT I *NEVER* RUN INTO AN *UGLIER* NEUTER-BOOTER THAN...

HEY...

EASY...

DOWN BOY!...

A MERE JEST! HEH... HEH...

CRATER FACE...

HEY, HARRY! WHOOZE THE MOUTH?

THIS IS THE FIRST AR'N'AR I'VE HAD IN THREE RIGONS! I'M *ALLOWED!*

AM I *RIGHT?*

HEY!

I'M *DEHYDRATIN'* OVER HERE! SHAKE YOUR CIRCUITS AN' SHIFT GEARS ON OVER HERE BEFORE THAT *ASS* LOCKS ON YOU!

ANYBODY EVER HEAR ABOUT THE MORE THAN USUALLY *BUILT* PLEASURE DROID?

HEY!

I'M TALKIN' *GUT-BUSTER!!!*

HOHOHOHO!

THEY GAVE HER AN ORDER TO "HAUL-ASS" AN' IT TOOK HER *THREE* TRIPS!

THREE TRIPS! HEY! HEY!

THERE WERE THESE...

HEY! YOU WITH THE MOUTH IN HYPERDRIVE! MUFFLE YOUR JETS!

...TWO ANDROMEDICONES AND... HUH? ...DID I *HEAR* SOMETHIN'?

WUZ THAT A SMART REMARK OR JUST A *LITTLE MOUSEY* FARTIN' IN THE VOID? I *WONDER* WHAT THAT COULDA BEEN?

THE LAST TIME I HEARD A VOICE LIKE THAT, IT WAS WHISTLIN' OUTOFA *PIG'S* REAR!

"GALATIA NINE, FREELANCE FIGHTER ...PLEEZED TA MEET YA!"

"THE PLEASURE, I AM *QUICK* TO ASSURE YOU, IS ALL MINE. HEY! *GREAT* OUTFIT! LOVE THE SPIKES ...VERY DANGEROUS."

"HE-E-E-Y... CHECK IT *OUT*... THERE'S A MAN WHO *KNOWS* HOW TO FILL A PRESSURE SUIT... WHATSAY WE MOSEY OVER... MAYBE HE'S GOT A FRIEND?"

"I HAVE BETTER THINGS TO DO THAN BOOT AROUND THE PEENY PALACES WITH A VACUUM-SKULLED, SINGLE-STAGED BUBBLE HOPPER! AND *YOU* LOOK LIKE A WOMON WHO'D RATHER FIGHT THAN BITE YOURSELF."

"I'VE GOT A GOOD BERTH FOR A STRONG-ARMED, LEVEL-HEADED HUSTLER WHO'S SEEN A BIT OF THE GALAXY!"

"WHAT'S THE FARE?"

"DOWN THE HATCH BEFORE THEY BLOW A HOLE IN THE BAR."

"≡ I ALWAYS SAVE THE CHASER 'TIL AFTER THE KICK... ≡"

"THERE'S A MAN WHO *KNOWS* HOW TO MAKE A LADY SMILE!"

"COMMON, HANSOME, WANNA GET LUCKY?"

"*WHO'S* YOUR FRIEND?"

"BRU, MEET HARRY PALMER."

HEY, HARRY! HARRY PALMER? HARRY *PALM*-ER! HEH-HEH-HEH

...OH... GET IT?

HAIRY PALM?

SO WHAZIT GONNA BE?

RZZZ?

HUH?

PLAYIN' GOOSY-GANDER THRU THE ASTEROID BELT'S NO JOB FOR AN EX-BRIGADER!

BRIGADE? HOW DID YOU...

COM'ON, KID! HOT SUNS, HOT GUNS, THREE SQUARES A DAY AND A CHANCE TO MOVE UP IN THE RANKS!

♪ CLOSE *RANKED* WE STAND WITH *ARMS* OF GOLD, 'NEATH *BANNERS* BLUE OF HUE... ♪

NERF?

YEAH, KID, TRUE BLUE-- WHADDYA SAY? PLENNY OF WORK FOR A HOT TRIGGER FINGER ABOARD THE HARPY...

♪ THE *CHILDRED* OF EARTH'S FINEST MOLD, CLEAR-*EYED*, BRAVE *HEARTS* AND *TRUE*!! ♪

≥Snif≤

CLEAR-EYED?

I GOTTA GO PAWN A WATCH, HARRY. TAKE CARE OF BRUNHILDA HERE TILL I GET BACK...

♪ AMERCA-A-A-A-A-A-A-A-DIA! THE *HOMELESS* SING YOUR *HYMN*...! ♪

MOTHER, MY HEAD...

♪ AMER*CA-A-A-A-A-A-A*-DIA! BRIGHT *JEWEL* NEVER *DIMMED!* ♪

≈SNIF≈

...BASTARDS.

I'LL JUST RING UP THOSE DRINKS ON *YOUR* TAB, GALATIA.

TAB? WHUZZAT.... *I'M* BUYIN' THE DRINKS, I SAID. HELL, I'M *PAYIN'* THE *TAB,* TOO. C'MON.... *ADD* 'EM UP! THE *WORKS!* *BRUCILLA'S* PAYIN' THE FREIGHT!

IF YOU SAY SO.... CATCH YA LATER, HARRY.

GRT...

B-A-LLA-AM!

I RECONSIDERED YOUR MOST KIND *OFFER,* CAP!

UH.... GLAD TO HAVE YOU ABOARD, BRU.

OH....UH.... *CAP?* I FEEL I SHOULD SAY THAT YOU NEGLECTED TO *MENTION* THAT YOU BEEN RUNNIN' UP THAT *TAB* FOR THE PAST *SIX* CYCLES....

YOU NEGLECTED TO ASK.

TOUCHÉ, CAP.... YOU GOTTA POINT THERE.... AN I HOPE YOU ALSO HAVE SOME *CREDITS,* CAUSE YOUR *BAR* TAB HAS *BUSTED* BRUCILLA FLATTER THAN A *KANSAS* KORNKAKE.

CREDITS? DID I HEAR YOU SAY *CREDITS?* I GOTTA DEAL YOU CAN'T BEAT.

SAY WHAT?

IN A WORD.... PLATINUM.

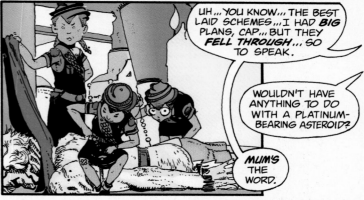

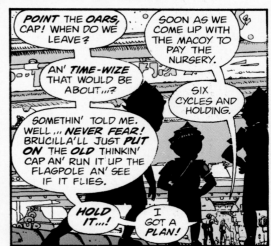

THE PLAN

SEE IT *NOW!* ONLY A QUA-CREDIT! COULD BE YOUR LAST CHANCE!

STAND *BACK,* *ALLA* YA!

GIMME SOME *ELBOW* ROOM OR END UP WITH *DEEP-FRIED* RETINAS, *TAKE* YOUR *PICK!*

...EAST EXIT...?

YOU SLOBS ARE ABOUT TO WITNESS A *FASCINATIN'* DISPLAY OF *SKILL* AND *PRECISION,* SO GET READY AND HOLD *TIGHT* TO YOUR *TAILS,* AN' YA WON'T LOSE 'EM.

COUNT 'EM!

STAND READY!

TAKE YOUR AIM!

BLAST ASS!

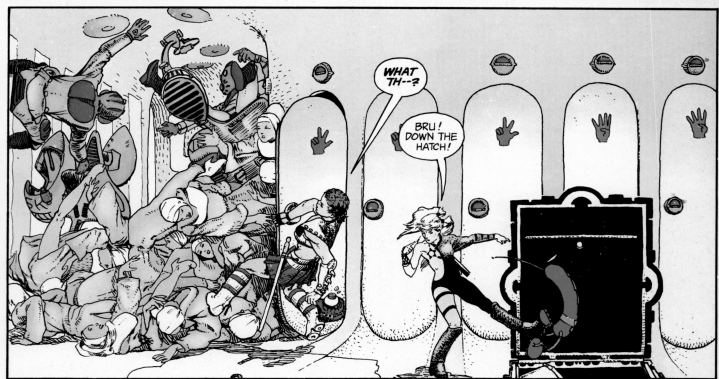

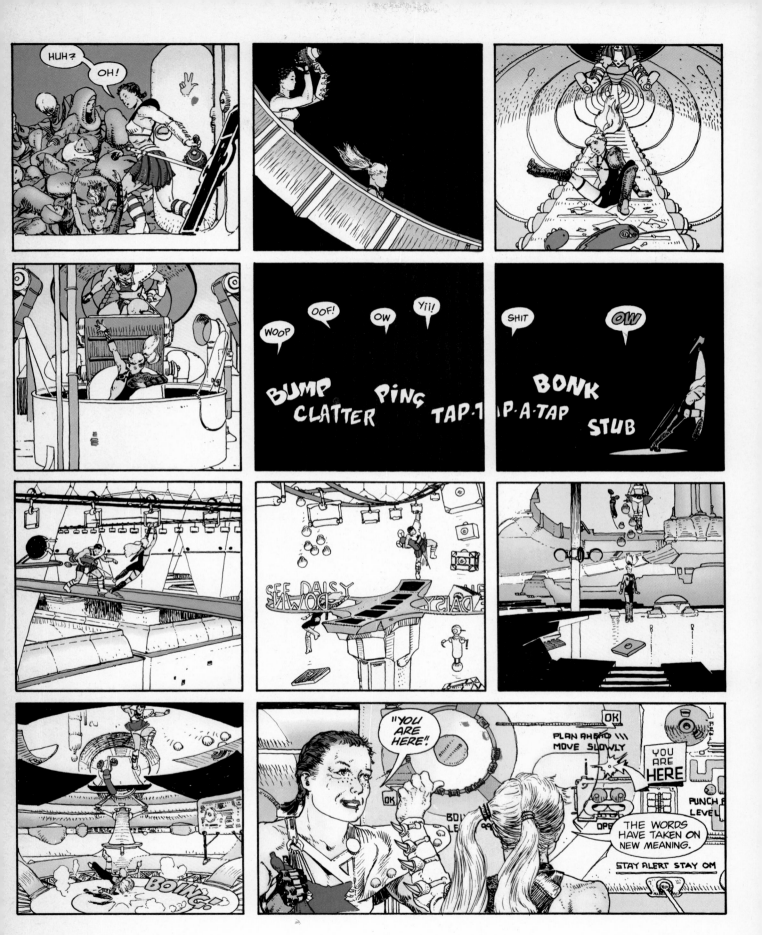

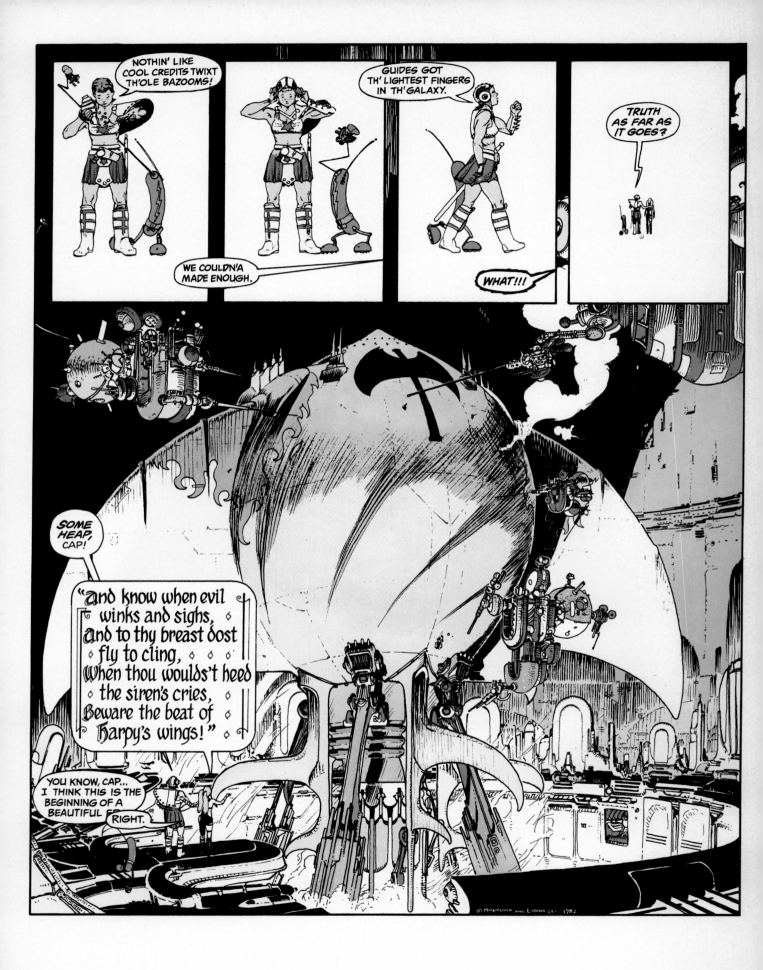

MAMMYGRAM™ [CONT. FROM PRIOR TOO-UNIT] SUBJECT GROUP AGAIN ON BLUE HEAVEN. GUIDES ENGAGED IN S.C.A.M. STAGE FINI: DIVEE THE SWAG. REAL McCOY!

GUIDES PROCEED DOWN...

HOLY COW!

GUIDES PROCEED DOWN...

PRIORITY OVERRIDE! REQUEST AUDIENCE!

SQUEEEEEE!!

DO YOU HAVE ANY IDEA WHAT TIME IT IS HERE?

AN EROTICA ANN DROID... MINT CONDITION... SEEMINGLY INVOLVED IN THE GUIDES' S.C.A.M....

FORGET THE GUIDES! GRAB THE DROID!

IT'S IMPORTANT!!!

THANKS FOR COMING, MAMA. LET ME BORROW YOUR HANKIE.

TRUEHEART

KLIK!

THAT'S RIGHT...THE YOUNG LIEUTENANT WHO DELIVERED YOUR DEAR, BRAVE JESERIT INTO DEATH'S DARK EMBRACE ...REC 97.

...YES, ON REC 97...THE NANCONTH FAMILY...VENGEANCE...THE YOUNG BRIGADER *YOU* SET UP...AND HOW *IS* YOUR SON...

...THE ONE THAT HANDED WEATHERAL YOUR VITALS RESTING ON A BED OF *STANDARD CREDITS*...UH-HUH...97. JUST THOUGHT YOU'D LIKE TO KNOW...

...A TIP...THE TWO FEMFIGHTERS WHO "BLEW" HEAVEN AND THE BOTTOM OUT OF PLATINUM...IN THE NURSERY... SOON TO BLOW SKY HIGH...

...THIS SHOULD TICKLE THE OLE "FAMILY" JEWELS...SPOTTED AN *ANNIE* IN MINT CONDITION! IN THE COMPANY OF A SAILOR...ONE BREAST... BELT HIGH...SCAR...REC 97.

...HAVE YOU HUGGED YOUR DROID TODAY? FIND GALATIA 9 AND THAT *MOTOR-MOUTHED MINER*... "NURSING" THEIR BIRDIE...

...LADY SANDANKO...A MESSAGE FOR PRIME MINISTER GLORIANNA... "TWO OF HER KITTENS HAVE LOST THEIR--"

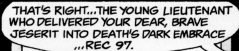

I'LL TAKE THAT.

SO...INDIRA LUCREZIA RONNIE LEE ELLIS BAJAR... WHAT DO YOU THINK THIS IS, *AMATEUR NIGHT?*

THE STARSTRUCK GLOSSARY

Americadian Space Brigade, The

The military arm of Amercadia. Shortly after the Unification of Sovereign Townships ended the only longish period of peace in Old Terran History, the associated governments of the United States and Canada (now Amercadia) began to wonder what THEY were up to. All the little home guards were made into one big HOME GUARD. Its chief function was to protect Amercadia from EVERYBODY IN THE WORLD. When NOBODY came, Amercadia began to have bigger worries. If THEY weren't coming from the other side of the globe, there was a good chance THEY were coming from OUT THERE. Amercadia mobilized a great space fleet. Brave lads and lasses were "recruited" into the new Amercadian Space Brigade and sent OUT THERE. Their chief function was to protect Amercadia from EVERYBODY. Once they got OUT THERE, they discovered that no one had even the slightest interest in Amercadia. Having been robbed of their reason d'etre, they pondered the alternatives. They adapted. Their chief function became PRESERVE AND SUSTAIN THE BRIGADE. The Brigade prospered and grew, trading its military might to an ally HERE for…oh let's say Borinyum Krystals…becoming involved in a small conflict THERE and being repaid by an OH-SO-GRATEFUL government with a tiny shipment of monopoles. Amercadia ITSELF became less and less a real place and more and more an Ideal of the Brigade. AMERICADIA's chief function became FEED THE BRIGADE.

ArcheOrganaApocolypsia

By all accounts, the worst play ever produced, ArcheOrgana-Apocolypsia traces the humanoid race from its humble beginnings, to its predicted destruction (see: Brand New Testament, The) Each performance lasted a full nargon and was presented in three acts: The Creation, The Duration, The Devastation. The play was written by Brother Anthony Quantis, playboy theologian and ex-member of the Brothers of the Dangling Zed, a heretical Christo-Zedian sect. It was re-written and staged by well known director, Sambo Thrace-Smythe. In the words of Onus Wren, renowned theatre critic, "A futile exercise in intellectual auto-eroticism. Better by far had he (Thrace-Smythe) inserted a trisone injectible into his left ear."

ArcheOrganaApocolypsia resulted in the financial devastation of anyone even slightly involved with the production and, less directly, the deaths of the Troikani actors, Personus/Ex/Mahkina and the well known director, Sambo Thrace-Smythe.

Cosmic Veil, Cloistered Order of the

Of the myriad religions in the known Universe, the Cloistered Order of the Cosmic Veil is the only one with no splinter factions, hence, it is easily definable by its own tenets which are as follows: 1) The Mother is Paradox; Ever Present and Never There when you need HER, 2) Non-Participation is the better part of Action, 3) If the Pond is Illusion, then what are the Ripples? 4) All Things come to She who Waits…and waits…and waits …5) Confuse Karma; Stand quite still and think of Nothing. The cloisters, which are scattered about the more densely populated regions, are round in shape, small in size, and packed full to union with the Void…or so they say. Certain socioarcheologists have pointed to the similarities between the tenets of the Cosmic Veil and the tenets of the Daughters of the Drowning Isis, a fictional religion introduced in the best selling *Mind Spiders from the Planet Xenon,* by the Hugo Award winning author, Ronnie Lee Ellis.

Galactic Girl Guides

On my honor I will do my best to do my duty to the Mother and to my Universe, to help other Girl Guides whenever doing so does not conflict with my own best interest, and to obey, if possible, the Girl Guide Law—Galactic Girl Guide Pledge.

An organization dedicated to the schooling of young girls in survival tactics on a galactic scale, the

GALATIA 9

Galactic Girl Guides trace their roots to Pre-Unification Amercadia. They began as the Junior Girl Guard, a branch of the Home Guard of the Sovereign Township Kansas. The Girl Guard served as a training ground for future Kansan patriots (see: Space Rangers) and, according to the Official Galactic Girl Guide Handbook, was "probably okay if you fancy being bullet bait for a bunch of blowhard bigshots who could care less if you got your tail kicked forty ways from Sunday." The Guard was immensely popular and soon spread to other Sovereign Townships in what was soon to become Amercadia. Their popularity dwindled during The Unification and the nationalization of the HOME GUARD. This was due, in part, to a lack of funding and to the fact that most of the J.G.G.'s leadership had been drafted into the new Amercadian HOME GUARD. Their common sense outlook and grassroots ideals remained close to the hearts of Amercadians, however, and during the early Expansion, they resurfaced. They broke their ties with what had been the HOME GUARD and was now the Amercadian Space Brigade and advertised themselves as a school-of-hard-knocks that prepared young girls to cut the mustard in a tough galaxy "It's a TOUGH GALAXY..." read the recruiting posters, "...but SOMEBODY'S gotta live in it. It might as well be YOU!" And from the Official Galactic Girl Guide Handbook, "A Girl Guide is wary, cunning, clever, assertive, flexible, patient, inventive, and brave but not stupidly so." The Guides belonged to a small group or "wing" and were classified by age as Chickadees, Jaybirds, Blackbirds, and Senior Guides or Voidettes. The coveted title Hawk Class Guide was an earned only position.

Today's Guides are part of a Galaxy-wide net of 5,300,487 wings. The Guides are very loosely connected to each other through the 3G Mobile Galactic Headquarters and Campground. They work their way up in the ranks by acquiring merit badges. Some examples are: The Do-Yo-Stuff badge, awarded for escaping punishment when caught in the act. This badge is sometimes accompanied by the "Silver Tongued Sister" badge if the guide manages to turn the situation entirely around in her favor so that she escapes with honor and awards. There are shark badges (card, pool, dark-bone-mark), a stowaway badge, and the highly prized "Sign of the Nova" badge which is awarded for deceiving the Girl Guide staff into awarding you at least 52 badges you haven't earned. This very useful education has created a great demand for guide-trained women. They make terrific corporate spies, professional gamblers, and hostess bouncers at some of the rougher leisure spots. Finally, the spirit of the Galactic Girl Guides is summed up in their motto: "TRUTH AS FAR AS IT GOES."

Kublacaine

An ego-enhancing drug that takes hold of a normal (or sub-normal) ego, foundering in the umbra of rational thought, id-ridden, fumbling, and unaware of it or idself, and transforms it into a forged titanium fortress housing a crystalline consciousness just dripping with highlights and bristling with juicily dangerous sharp edges. The subject remains calm, outwardly, while within burgeons a bigger and Oh-So-Very-Calmer calm...a waveless calm...a serene reposeful, halcyonian calm...a calm based on the sudden and irrefutable knowledge that one is really quite a great guy...a prince in fact ...Nay! A Lord! A GREAT LORD, STARK AND TERRIBLE, WHOSE NAME OR INTIMATION OF HIS NAME CONJURES OVERAWE AND SOLEMN VENERATION IN EACH MERE AND MORTAL CONSCIOUSNESS WITHIN THE VAST BREADTH OF ONE'S OMNISCIENT GAZE! FAINT HEARTS QUAIL! ALL BOW...NAY, GENUFLECT BEFORE THE ALL KNOWING, ALL SEEING, ALL BEING BEING!

Outwardly, as we've stated, one remains calm. One tipples a beverage, disturbs the nap of the rug with a languorous toe, flicks a speck of mortal coil from one's.

cuff, sighs, stifles a well-deserved yawn of nascent ennui while one's golden thoughts caress the dulcifluous knowledge that one's oafish acquaintances, ne'er-do-well relatives, interfering in-laws, insensible siblings, impaired parents, gross supplicants and servile hangers on, the family dog and the whole fam damnily of humanoid-kind, along with their wives, husbands, sisters, cousins, clones, droids, pets and parasites and the countless rat-like embryos of the cosmos at large and their crawling, toady alien counterparts exist ONLY AT ONE'S WHIM...craving only a nod...a wink...a kick...to feel elevated for but an instant above the meaningless morass of their own near-lives. Kublacaine is the pinnacle, head-wise.

Needless to say, it comes in mighty handy on an intersteller jaunt of any great distance. Puts it all in its proper perspective.

Neutral Zones

During the Expansionist Era, the first Neutral Zone was declared shortly after two Amercadian Scouts were lost in the vicinity of Barnards Star. The last recorded communication from the ship (The Beaver) still echoes echoes echoes down the hollow arm of Father Time.

    Rongschilde: Sure is quiet...?
    Jones: Yeah...too quiet.

By the early days of IER, any slice, hunk, wedge, or space of space deemed responsible for three verified disappearances of sentient beings became a lawfully designated Neutral Zone. Verification Recordings, Neutral Zone 8: 1) "It's AMAZING! IT'S FANTASTIC!!! IT'S...IT'S..." (static). 2) "I see a...I see...I..." (static). 3) "These reports musta been fakes. This place is as safe as a..." (static). As the concept of Neutral Zones caught on, some beings found it convenient to augment the ruling to fit other situations. Areas of dispute plagued by border wars (where there was no real profit motive) soon became Neutral Zones, saving wear and tear on the Borderees. This ruling was enforced by Expansionist and later IER Authorities in an effort to quiet troubled trade areas. Toward

the end of the Stagnation, PAHM Bajar began an experiment using Vercadian Protector Androids to defend the Zones. During the early Anarchera cycles (when, for all practical purposes there WERE NO authorities), the incredibly dangerous, incredibly expensive Vercadian Protector Androids became the chief means of enforcing Neutral Zones. If you were rich enough to have a droid, you could have a Zone.

Thrace-Smythe, Sambo

Well-known director famous for producing very long works with very long names and of a quasi-religious nature. Little is known of his early life. He left the Boones Dock Academy of Speech and Drama in AE 23 after having lost his scholarship to an unknown performance artist. With the aid of an obsolete Miz-Fix-it droid (see: Handy-Andi) and a Thia-line Drone, he captured a Rootersnoos Beacon in the Noh Zone and began broadcasting the cult classic radio series, "WHY?" "WHY?!!!" the voice echoed electronically down the back streets of the galaxy, "...OR BLOWN FROM THE ASS OF GOD! The continuing adventures of Perplexus Eqs Youth! (dramatic music) Journey with me to the thrilling daze of yestercycle, when magic was real and every new beginning had a new name. (more dramatic music) My name? (ditto) Just call me...(echo effect) A CRY IN THE NOTHINGNESS!!!" By the time Rootersnoos discovered what was going on and sent someone to check it out, the void-space surrounding the beacon was packed out to 58 sparlons with the ships and stellar-copters of loyal fans that looked, from a distance, like a school of Aguatunesian Tuna. "WHY" was syndicated, Thrace-Smythe, an overunit success. Between AE 29 and 92, he would write, produce, and direct more that 50 plays including PARAPLEGIA, META-MORPHICA, METAPHORIA, and the enormously successful AERIO-PAGITICA. Between Cycles 93 and 120 he became disillusioned and depressed and did his famous "blue period" work, the eternally

BRUCILLA AS A KRABIAN SLAVE

running soap opera, CYCLES IN-FINITUM and the silly but financially rewarding musical, LET GO AND LET GOD! In Cycle 128, Thrace-Smythe staged what·was, by all accounts, the worst play ever produced ... ARCHEORGANA-APOCOLYPSIA. Due to the public humiliation and the outcry at the ritual deaths of the Troikani actors Personus/Ex/Mahkina, Thrace-Smythe went underground for 9 cycles and emerged in AE 137 as a director of lasarounds. He directed 13 lasarounds and then disappeared mysteriously at the opening of his 14th, PHOENIX-FLOWEROTICA, (based on Lotti Bo Sugar's best selling autobiography, HOW I INADVERTENTLY STUMBLED INTO A SCIENTIFIC BREAKTHROUGH AND WAS BLINDED.) He was never seen again. One explanation of his disappearance can be found in Kettle Black's controversial play, THE PERSECUTION AND ASSASSINATION OF SAMBO THRACE-SMYTHE AS PERFORMED BY THE MEMBERS OF THE GUERNICAN ART SQUAD UNDER THE DIRECTION OF TERONIA TA or THRACE-SMYTHE/TA. During the course of the play, Black (playing herself) recreates the scene in which she and two other members of the squad capture Thrace-Smythe. He is murdered horribly and his emotional essence, preserved at the last mili-ribec of his life, is bottled by "BRUSH AND BLASTER" (the Art Squad's mercenary division) and sold as their famous "EMOTIONAL COLORS #3, ANGST & AGONY." Emotional colors are mixed with any pigment and add to a finished painting a palpable aura of feeling.

Troikani

The people of Troika (both singular and plural). A Troikani has an extremely flexible persona, a very shallow id, and almost NO sense of self. It takes the hearts, minds, and souls of AT LEAST three Troikani to make even ONE respectable psyche. Even so...they can quickly adapt to the most extreme environment, melt quietly into the strangest of cultures, and mimic ANYTHING, creature or

concept, in the known universe. They make excellent actors. When left alone, without the company of others of its species, a Troikani will have one of three reactions: 1) It will pine away and die, 2) It will run through its entire repertoire of roles (these collected over a lifetime) at a speed incredible to behold until dead from exhaustion, 3) It will call the actors' union every marbec on the marbec to complain about *everything* in the known universe until the union sends someone to put it out of its misery.

Vercadian Protector Android

The ony android culture (or batch) capable of premeditated assault on a sentient being...the Cyberphobe's nightmare. They are incredibly expensive and incredibly dangerous. Vercadian Protector Androids were built in the early Cycles of IER-CO by the Vercadian Andromedicones in an effort to 1) fulfill their programming by providing a nearly indestructible protector for its human owners, 2) to "scratch an old itch" by providing humankind with yet another means of destroying itself, and 3) to bring home the bacon. Lots and lots of bacon. Standard features include Atomo-Torch Power Gauntlets, thought activated body shield, Pec-Flex Implosion-Head Destructo-Dart System, Rear Guard atomic cannon, boot tip disemboweling horns, adjustable vanity mirror, Chakra-Rocket Id-Seeking Quasar Bullets, and Switz Armsy Guards with gutting, slicing, and filleting knives (tweezers optional). The two best known and most feared of all Vercadian Protector Androids were Veep 7, the warrior-poet, and 785, the gold-plated bodyguard of the Mayor of Casterbridge. An old children's tale tells of Veep 7, the masterless droid, that he was once stared down by a chinchilla from the Yndokrin Mining Belts and so lost his arm guard.

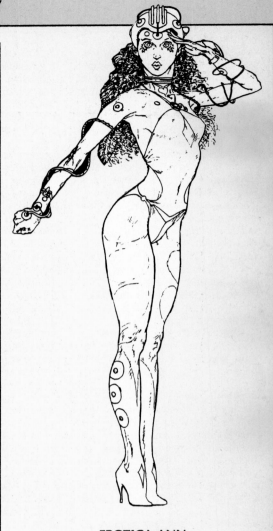

EROTICA ANN